I0156606

ORPHEUS
IN OUR WORLD

New Poems on Timeless Forces

Patricia Keeney

NeoPoiesisPress.com

NeoPoiesis Press, LLC

2775 Harbor Ave SW, Suite D, Seattle, WA 98126-2138
Inquiries: Info@NeoPoiesisPress.com
NeoPoiesisPress.com

Orpheus in our World: New Poems on Timeless Forces
ISBN 978-0-9975021-2-1 (pbk)

1. Poetry. I. Keeney, Patricia.

Library of Congress Control Number: 2016915432

First Edition

Cover Design: Milo Duffin and Stephen Roxborough

Printed in the United States of America.

For Gina

Introduction

This book began one warm evening in Athens, when the Plaka rang with voices and laughter. Over grilled octopus and frosty retsina I found myself in animated conversation with my good friend Regina Kapetenakis. Former Chorus Director for the National Theatre of Greece and deeply committed to the Greek classics, Gina was excited about a new work for dance theatre. The Orphic Hymns, she exclaimed excitedly, had not yet been 'done' in modern times. She went on to declare that I, as a poet must 'adapt' them. Why? Because these packed explosions of lyric intensity were relatively unknown and begged for new interpretation. The fact that they existed most purely in classical Greek shouldn't worry me since Gina knew the ancient language and would 'translate.'

When I protested that my only knowledge of Orpheus centred around the doomed singer, enchanter of nature and lover of Euridyce who, when trying to rescue her from Hades, dared to gaze upon her and for this transgression was ultimately torn to pieces by the Maenads, Gina replied, there was a book I must read.

Called *The Orphic Hymns: Astronomy in the Age of Ice* by Siegfried Pyrrhus Petrides, it explored the navigational and astronomical skills of the ancient Greeks, proposing a theory that explained how the name 'Orpheus' developed. It was a title, according to Petrides, taken by the first priest/astronomer. Eventually, "Orphic" followers united under this name that came to signify both the star-gazer and the hymn-singer. Indeed, "Orphic" sanctuaries of some 10,000 years ago were astronomical observatories, which as well as looking "outward," also looked "inward," creating hymns to the Hellenic gods and goddesses.

A painstaking and exuberant reclamation of arcane knowledge, Petrides' book salvages and contextualizes these early Greek hymns in a heroic feat of scholarship and sustained enthusiasm.

Through Petrides, we touch the religion of the ancient Hellenes: hymns to the evolution of life in cosmological and psychological terms, hymns that take us through the earliest expressions of creation, of time and of power. We witness the birth of the first gods, the multiplication of the gods, their extension through time, and ultimately their power over human affairs, both individual and global. Throughout the journey, we observe the ancient manifestations of cosmic elements, such as earth, air and night; abstract concepts such as justice or fate; human traits personified, such as love or grief.

What appealed to me was the combination of science and mythology, the naming of natural forces and phenomena, the personal invocation made through vivid metaphors that picture the power and beauty of the physical world: Poseidon, earth-shaker, dark-haired one; Demeter with the splendid fruits; Hermes the herald. Here was an inclusive poetry of life energy, a fusion of science and art forging highly charged speculative fictions. *Orpheus in our Time* attempts to re-cast the hymns as the lyric poems they truly are.

Permission to do so is given, by Petrides himself in his own disclaimer: not a poet, he challenged "anyone endowed with poetical inspiration" to "enhance" the work he had begun. I started with Petrides' original hymns in mostly literal translation from the ancient Greek, finding them rather frugal and often awkward. But exciting. The dense imagery hid universal secrets, inspiring revelations and re-visioning, if we could but listen. And hear. Once more.

The strength and sensuality I discovered felt so new that what began to emerge as well was a ghost dialogue between a **he** and a **she** (facets of myself?) commenting on the timeless tales told in these poems, sometimes free-associating around a name or a word that sends them rummaging through personal baggage, lazily daydreaming or occasionally soaring into new possibility. Alternately baffled and intoxicated by what they hear, **he** and **she** express current attitudes disposing them to re-consider various social, political and environmental issues, often from the prickly perspectives of male vs. female (in whatever gender those characteristics might appear). In their uncertain way, **he** and **she** navigate moments of their contemporary lives through chaos and calm, through poetry and practicality, humour and desperate question, much of it jointly unsettled and inspired by an un-named awareness.

Ancient voices. Contemporary voices. Everybody and nobody, alternately aroused and resigned. Where were we then? Where are we now? Without doubt, there is some force at work altering this "couple" caught as they are between the ancient music of Orpheus and the sensibilities of the 21st century, moving toward some brave new insight encouraging us to continue, through evolution, devolution and maybe even revolution into another way of being.

Here is a Petrides version of the hymn to Nike:

Hymn XXXIII. NIKE

Nike I invite the very powerful, much desirable to mortals,
Who's the only one relaxing mortals from the agonized impetus
And of the painful rivalries, in battles against adversaries.
Deciding in warfare operations, on the victorious outcomes,
to which when you are rushing upon bring a very sweet boast-
ing.
For you prevail over all; and the goodly result of every strife
deepens on you famous Nike, the winner celebrating frantically.
But, blessed, may you come with a desirable cheerful eye,
Bringing always to the renown deeds the fine glory.

Here is my version of the hymn:

Nike (Victory)
wave billower
wind shaker
earth trembler

stride down from the clouds
wingless among us
in hurricane garments
all fluttering muscle
hoverer, body of air
bent at the knee
to bind fast a sandal
sweet boaster

cheer us with knowing
all strife is joyful.

is life in its longing

and losing is winning

Here is the contemporary dialogue in response to the hymn:

he: what, going for gold?
you look like a fierce little boy in that outfit

she: turn you on?

he: if you're the prize

she: you've already won
trophy man, exhausted runner, let me
carry you home

he: I sense you before I see you
touch you, can't catch you

she: clipping my wings won't make me stay

he: ok you little speed sprite
but before you take off again
just…do up your laces

It is my hope that this re-imagining of the past will contribute to
the continuing life of these ancient hymns which might be read
again, visualized anew, danced, sung or even dramatized for the
first time. May Orpheus – the 'poet-saviour' – continue to work
his magic.

Patricia Keeney, Belvau, 2015

Contents

The First Gods

The Gods Multiply

Passing Through Time

Playing with Power

The First Gods

Physis (First Mover)

before you
nothing
parent of yourself
pre-existent
imperishable

supreme demon
glory giver
being's bellowing sergeant
booster and builder

endless line spinning top

big creator solo maker

firing up fate
along wisdom's wise flow

trembling the sceptre and fixing the throne
king and queen of possibility

you dancing inventor
circling yourself
feet silent on soil

nursing what's not
nourishing what needs
to be

unchanging changer

he: change frightens me

she: it excites me

he: I must plan. don't like surprises

she: I enjoy the unpredictable

he: why?

she: it's interesting
　　　not knowing is interesting

he: but then you can't be prepared

she: I like to improvise, test my resourcefulness

he: you live dangerously

she: I'd say adventurously and besides

　　　our world demands we adapt
　　　otherwise we're doomed

3

Protogonus (Firstborn God)

pulsing egg, afloat in the ether
burst from your cell
golden-winged and bull-eyed

sperm-spray the whirling world

rocket down
to our garden of plenty
silent and shining

erect and un-aging in time

she: remember Provence
on the balcony over the cherry orchard

he: looking at you
bare by the pool

she: your shower of love
spilled down through the sun

he: a moment of true
divinity

Gaia (Earth)

matter mere matter
all matter

earth is the matter
deathless

spinner of stars
flower-faced demon
smiler in the rain

heal us through pain

load up your lap with beginning

nurse our new forms
into being again

he: what is the matter?

she: dying
　　　the centre burns out
　　　　melts down

Ether (Air)

oceans I breathe
but can't see

beat of my being
continuing me

atoms brewing
bubbling in the pot

morsels of everything
always and everywhere
netted in air

web of fire

cosmic seed dust
drifting down

she: we're inhaling poison

he: messed up all
we were given

she: what do we do now?

he: nothing

she: we must try so hard
to do nothing

Nyx (Night)

night mother
flickering stars

dream mother
fostering feasts
           and sleep

earth mother
moving our lives between
darkness and light

        dance

  every day
     all the way
        down

 to the cave
     of your knowing

she: I'm restless

he: count sheep
    take a pill
    go blank

    just don't keep me
            awake

Eros (Desire)

thrusts it all together
sweet strong boy aiming fire

shaker and breaker
of body and mind

molder of two in one
wrestler of double to single

timeless

he: do you really feel that way
    that we're stuck like crazy glue?

she: there is something pre-destined about us

he: that's grand but we're talking a delinquent imp
    shooting impetuous arrows

she: no, we're talking gravitational pull

he: this could get messy

she: you're tearing me apart

he: don't you believe in us?

she: I've never felt so warm or right
    or
      timeless

The Gods Multiply

Uranus (the Cosmic Dance)

spin daddy spin

whirl around the world
your long bright ribbons
for every living thing

turn me loose and flutter me
pull me tight again

revolve yourself
devolve yourself

spin daddy spin

she: I'm bored

he: you're bored because you're not passionate about anything

she: what do you suggest?

he: do something drastic
involve yourself

Astra (Stars)

sharp lights
shivering children of night

blazing the ring
from beginning to end

holy eyes trawling
each dim veil

shaft of fire
striking and leaving

fire road runners
zoned clear

he: can you see stars?

she: no
       but I feel them
       we are...

he: what?

she: how do we bring them back?

he: turn off the lights
       and hold
              on

Boreas (North Wind)

king of the winds
top of the cold clock

blasting ice down
from a stiff spiked world

polishing sky

widening eyes in the glass
of your seeing

he: come sit by the fire and melt into me

she: let our minds slowly drip into spring

he: I want halcyon days
  to sit on sea rocks in a cradle of waves
  and hatch all our dreams into being

she: sing the winter winds to sleep

he: roll them up and put them away for the season

she: I long for warm rains tumbling blossom
  damp wings shuddering

Notus (South Wind)

damp air
flowers on the wing
pungent fluttering scents
playing with promise
heavy clouds heaving

pour down, pour down

strong dry puffing
little breezes weak and wet

burrow in

a giant bath, the sea
heats for Halcyon
dropping her eggs
off precipitous ledges

when massive moving air
stills, she sits
between summer and snow

hatching her future

NB: In Greek mythology, Halcyon was the daughter of Aeolus, god of winds. Because Halcyon had once shown disrespect to Zeus, she was turned into a bird sentenced to incubate its eggs during the winter and not during the spring like other birds. Building her nest on sea rocks, Halcyon was continually losing her chicks due to storm waves. Zeus felt sorry for her and offered her a break for fourteen quiet days.

she: not winter or spring

he: just a tease, ambivalent

she: like some people

he: why should we expect others
    to be what we want?

she: so disappointing when they aren't
    like the poet I admired
    eloquent, sensitive
    socially committed, fierce
    in his writing...
    suddenly diffident and shy
    ducking away like a bird in a gust
    glass-eyed, this tired old man
    all his strength spent
    on sad stories and need

he: expertly avoiding
    the vigorous, he knows

she: he will outlast us

Zephyrus (West Wind)

Air roamer, whisperer
breeze rower

puffing between us
your feathery vapours

fair draft always forward

beguiling to windlullers
windbedders
priests on a mountain
wafting the brave
from their burning

sprung free from the blustery bag
of big wings

slight wavering light

help us to harbours
and cradles of calm

NB: Windbedders and Windlullers were specialized priests whose
responsibility was the managing of the winds

he: your resentment
blows me out of the water

she: we're always storming
at each other

he: too much pressure
from every quarter
of our little globe

she: bouncing through space
like a rubber ball
world of wind
in a thimble

he: what do we leave
set free
our jobs, our children
each other?

she: we need to drop anchor
somewhere quiet
and consider

he: what must go
so we can stay

afloat

Eos (Dawn)

faint light
buried by night
push back blackness

slow glow seeping up
flush the dome warm

lift limbs, open eyes
wake up the work in us

send snakes coiling
tickle bugs alert
whisper fish through foam
uncurl all winged and walking things

pale sun door opening

he: my sleeping girl

she: stretch, baby, stretch

he: goddess rising, I want all of you

she: morning's the best time for love

Helius (the Sun)

sweet beast face
golden dawn and dusk

dance on your paws
run round your track
fire up all
cosmic harmony

lift flame
from flame

tame the colours
of your blissful eye

despot of waters

whip through world's weathers
justify us

he: a suntan is sexy

she: skin cancer is not

he: and vitamin D?

she: healthy of course

he: maybe healthy is sexy

she: what about love?

he: love is dangerous

Oceanus (First Water)

burst from earth and sky
river rope around the world

splash neat-ankled nymphs
far and deep, a giddy babble
as they flow
bubbling up sunsets

ferry fire back to morning

bathe the stars

wash us until
our divinity glows

grow back the god in us

she: how I hate buying swimsuits

he: dare I ask why?

she: stuffing in my skin

he: you have beautiful skin

she: not under fitting room lights

he: in the sun and the wind
and the sea, you're a mermaid

she: that's good. keep me in water
behind glass

Tethys (Waterways)

earth's daughter
sister of the ocean

dark-gowned lady
waving veils
breeze bound round the world

aid the ways of water

break against shores into shapes
that enchant us
froth white, slip and slide
on the islands we know

crystalline spirit
carry our dreams
all the places
you go

she: why don't you swim?

he: it's cold and wet
    I don't know what's below

she: it's buoyant and cool
    always gets through

he: yeah, floods, hurricanes and tsunamis

she: rivers and streams
    altering landscape
    through eons

he: oil slicks and dead fish

she: all the new islands we've yet to explore
    and worlds undersea

    such fabulous freedoms

Nereus and Nereides
(Old Man of the Sea and His Maidens)

wind-whipper
earth-shaker
dance with your daughters

blue-rooted in sea-beds
shudder the mirror

cascading on dolphins with each of your beauties
through doldrums and currents

ruffled and calm

speeding
      or still

she: oh how I'd love to be

he: what?

she: sea-born

he: maybe you are

she: fish-tailed and finned
sea-weedy tresses trailing you down
to breathe different air

he: sure, I'm ready

she: you're about as ready as kids
with water wings and a noodle

Hypnus (Sleep)

fatherless
son of night
death's brother

shadowed, filtering light
winged darkness, brushing
thought with oblivion's branch

loving the moon, wide-eyed

burying heroes

gliding over ground
pouring forgetfulness down
from your pitcher

of freedom

*

he: it must have been scary

she: a first for me, never sick
     then suddenly the engine stalls
     'broken heart' syndrome, they said

he: poetic

she: utterly helpless with tubes and pills

he: caused by?

she: stress

36

he: but we all...

she: there are hidden reservoirs
      subconsciously I opened a floodgate

he: wow!

she: the muscle stretched
      reversing some valve flow

he: what was the worst?

she: just before anaesthetic
      telling me they would
      jumpstart things again

he: like car cables

she: and asking if I had dentures
      because that could be dangerous
      I saw teeth clattering wildly around the room
      like a bad Halloween joke
      so I told them the only thing false
      was a little hair colour

he: bet they loved that

she: they did

he: and then?

she: then everything was ok

Oneiron (Dream Messenger)

whispering prophet
arriving in silence

mutely unveiling
the future

your eloquent images
breaths from the blessed

dissolving all anger and fear
exhausting death's dread

airy with promise

forming before us
the shapes that will carry us

through

he: do you dream?

she: only what I've lived
in some odd re-arrangement
but always more real
than the actual experience

he: a subconscious filtering process

she: our dinner last night
with your old critic friend
plump as a pincushion
wittily bristling
fuzzy white hair and ruddering laugh
in my sleep she was eighteen and furious
flaming whirlwind of questions and protest

he: your mind extracts what matters

she: what matters?

he: that you don't stop
dreaming

Mnemosyne (Memory)

sweet sleep singer
bind myriad ways
of imagining
in one warm bed

                    alert aware alive
                    keep us awake
                    with ourselves

our minds filled
with other

                    sight sound smell
                    a nest of hatchlings

flying on word wings
numbering needs

he: what's your most important faculty?

she: memory

he: why?

she: it tells me where I came from
reminds me who I am

he: but you're more than what you were

she: the future eats the past

he: memory is quicksand – you can suffocate

she: she's also a seductress
sealing the self around us

he: a tomb of mirrors

she: in animals she marks territory
knows where home is
the dance that keeps a species
going

he: and our instincts?

she: gone

Nemesis (Retribution)

Racing the sea-lanes
alert for imbalance

checking presumption
punishing cunning
beamed in on your searchlight

gauging excess on the tang of a breeze
round your own quiet island

finger in the wind

olive branch and figured bowl
crown of the huntress

shining scales
dazzling dark waves

fishing up fickleness
flipped on a line
stilled in the air

ruddering incoherence clear
toppling down arrogance

turreted only
in cities of sharing
shocked at the haughty

roll smooth
under your feet
the perfect sphere

we've spoiled

he: what are you ashamed of?

she: envy greed self-doubt
and you?

he: laziness anxiety bullying
the way I look

she: yet we seem so confident
to the world

he: who are we kidding?

she: it's the only way to accomplish anything

he: why are we ambitious?

she: so we can justify our existence

he: and if we don't?

she: we feel guilty

he: nemesis

she: the balancing act

Themis (Conscience)

Pure seed of Uranus
Gaia's best sprout

Flower faced, looking
for light seeking truth
through the night

Sealed as a snake
in your red-figured oracles
pythoness, tripod triumphant
leaf-laurelled, royal

ruled not

by convenient executive systems
of gain

touched by intention
awake with the moon

balanced as noon
in the beams
of your justice

she: how do we know
     when we're right?

he: best guess

she: I hate shrieking at the kids

he: they need boundaries
     you have limits

she: some slack is ok I guess
     it's always a negotiation isn't it

he: the birds know it
     one season at a time

she: singing crimson
     tender taupe
     alchemical gold

he: ecstatic red-winged black

Titans (Basic Instinct)

defeated ones
children of the first gods

banished ancestors
outlandish, moving ash

volcanoes chained beneath our feet
for murdering ecstasy

outlawed impulses long buried
rooted deeper than Hades

groping blindly up
towards disaster

he: we're not pure, are we
we don't come empty

she: we're everything that always was
the good and the bad
crawling climbing
floating flying

he: how are we not drowned, burned
dragged down with the biological baggage?

she: we have the power to resist
make choices

he: only based on what we recognize

she: I see the animal in you

he: so Grimm is good for kids, to know
those ogres and urges exist in us

she: that's power

he: but there will always be casualties
serial killers

she: sink or swim
we're on the Titanic

Tyche (Chance)

gentle resident of streets
and fine buildings

ultimate adapter, whirling in weathers
every direction life moves

ruddering the globe

cornucopia of ways
shake from your wings
each shade of dream and event

daughter of forethought, mother of means
adventuress probing the possible
blind to the regular snip of its shears
playing dice with time's random length

beginning and ending

she: do you believe in luck?

he: yes and timing

she: it's not pre-determined?

he: I don't think so
because that would pre-suppose some god
or other

she: then what makes it all go wrong?

he: free fall
we sway and plummet
through our own atmosphere

she: only after crash landing
can rational analysis happen

he: expectation filling in
like a child's colouring book

Thanatos (Death)

idling in neutral

pure time

held at the helm
keel-hauling body
scattering soul

untying the knot and flipping us free
to the fathomless circle of sleep

a force with no face
before the beginning
and after the end

healer absolute
jury and judge

faultless transformer

wood into fire
stone into sand

born of the night

ultimate hypnotist
drug of unknowing
relieving the ego

a squeeze of red flower
entreating oblivion

he: what is death?

she: a transformation of energy

he: I believe that

she: what if we've used it all up?

he: is that what you're trying to do?

she: must be, can't seem to stop

he: what drives you?

she: the need to be here, now
     fully present

he: you can exist nowhere else
    in no other form?

she: if I can, I don't know it

he: I do

Passing Through Time

Cronus (Time)

father evergreen
root and branch strung out
through the cosmos

trapped in the world
for us to pluck and play

wit and word stretched
out of your head
so we might go on

seed of our being
inventor of measure
weaving shape and substance
from a thorny thought

carving up emptiness
with precision flint

she: wouldn't you like to know
a time before time
when we didn't count
days with numbers
names with fingers

he: when we always
had enough

she: time is
the tyrant that keeps us here

and cuts us off

Hecate (Queen of the Underworld)

smoking on the streets
spanning at the crossroads
splendid in saffron

billow my solitude

mother of dogs
running with deer
keeper of keys

unlock me now

he: she sits before a mirror
applying lipstick

she: bloodied, her face
screams back

Rhea (Engenderings)

god's mother
lightning-wombed
lion-pulled

bearer of round divinity
wearing your snake apron

drum-beater
shield-clasher

shake your hissing heads
against our troubles

cry over mountains
of mortals at war
weep in the wind

under skies of your smile

wake

        in a cave full of fire
        melting the ages
        of ice

she: suppose I give birth to a monster

he: or a marvel
    you begin life

she: it roars through me, ruining
    I will die

he: or start a dynasty

Aphrodite (Love)

scatter smiles
dark over loam
spill seed from the chariot
bath of your pleasures

liquidly linking safe and strange

love's warrior queen
soldier of seduction

worshipped by whores and political wives

giddy garden girl
dabbling with fertility

stirring deep beds in ocean and earth

whipping the waves
in round dances of water

leaping on beaches
lurching in wombs

sea-dazzled woman surging and sperm-soaked
blinded by spume

closer to sun than we
can ever be

why do you hide?

lost night and day
so alive

at the edges
of light

she: they say orgasm is merely
    muscle spasm

he: yes

she: it's world muscle

    the whole globe flinches
    then flares open

he: balloons

she: I balloon
    want to consume
    pull you all the way
    in

he: so I look out through your eyes
            me in you
            curved and curly
            strolling all the countries
            you contain

she: my body is the planet
    you have probed for

    is the planet you will land on
    and name

Nike (Victory)

wave billower
wind shaker
earth trembler

stride down from the clouds
wingless among us
in hurricane garments
all fluttering muscle

hoverer, body of air

bent at the knee
to bind fast a sandal
sweet boaster

cheer us with knowing
all strife is joyful
is life in its longing

and losing is winning

he: what, going for gold?
        you look like a fierce little boy in that outfit

she: turn you on?

he: if you're the prize

she: you've already won
         trophy man, exhausted runner, let me
         carry you home

he: I sense you before I see you
             touch you, can't catch you

she: clipping my wings won't make me stay

he: ok you little speed sprite
         but before you take off again
         just...do up your laces

Eumenides (Vengeance)

furious graces
spore from the core
of darkness, sprouting
god-dropped blood

sunk in your misty cave
border guards of the fire line
stuck by the perilous door
over what roars under us

daughters of Hades
tempered in fire, airborne
like angels or illness

your glittering faces
carry out curses
light up the blind beggar night

queens of the outcast
flying dead souls
in the snakes of your hair

writhing and shining

wise wily water flow
wash our names clear

as we fall

he: you get so angry

she: something
      lives so black and loud
      at home inside me

he: keep them out

she: they creep under my mind
      gnaw at the edges of reason
      break me down gently
      worry dreams stopping sleep

he: what is worry, why do we...

she: problems we can't solve
      frustration from the wrongs
      we can't right

      the fear that our individual existence
      doesn't improve anything

      my fury
      restores a balance

he: and destroys
                me

Demeter (Grieving Mother)

tread through the fields in straight rows
harness the oxen, drop seed as you go
into dark earthen beds

where girls sleep in their hiding:
your young ones who wait
preparing to bloom

don't dare touch my daughters
you raper and ravisher
do not pluck their petals
from faces of flowers

poppies and torches flare through the wheat fields

a disappearing deity
searching the seasons
for children who vanish

he: be my goddess of the corn
    my sower and reaper
    thresher and keeper
    underground mistress
    who'll save me from starving
    abuse

    be my madam of plenty
    silky hair and succulent nibblets
    winnow the wheat from my chaff

she: Undying, I change and renew
    for your torment

Hera (Wife)

flourishing woman
blue-winged and breezy

bird lord on your sceptre
red-chambered many-seeded
pomegranate orb

nursing new brides into marriage
where the river runs fast

joining dividing

gust of your rain
sweep of your breath
filling female lives

rising emptying dying

lie with him in your garden bed
watered by waves
garlands of animals weaving around
    ox-eyed
        sleek hide

urging the feats of young girls
racing and leaping
embracing

the all-mother prize

he: will you be...

she: not without a pre-nup

      but feel free to eat
             my love

he: you want security

she: I do

he: you don't
     trust me, need
     an escape clause

she: don't be romantic

he: we deserve each other

Hestia (Home Fires)

keep them lit

shape-shifter
flickering all ways
common as grass

low round hearth
navel of the royal rooms

mother comfort
of the civic system

middle woman, house bound

shining small flames
on new colonies
all tending their own
warm embers
with babies and brides

fat sacrifice
offered lavishly

sitter at the centre

veiling our pollution
rekindling our purity

burning, burning

he: to be everywhere
without moving
the bard - whoever he was -
said it: 'just imagine'

she: I must
experience to know

he: some never leave home

she: the whole globe is mine
familiar as that

he: look at the child
an Olympic champion
alone in her own
terra incognita

she: sunglasses in the mirror
stranger to herself

he: our house is her world

she: but she'll grow
and go

one must want children

Playing with Power

Zeus (Father God)

undoer of time
breaker of bonds
curl up
    unfurl

everything new from your head

animate sky
polish the air with weathers of self

minding who walks beyond borders

cloud-piler rain-maker fire-shooter
marksman of fame riding the bolts
of your javelin flame

a shuttle through space
sucking out sight
from the eye of the sea

cracking small shells of pure sound

in the sigh of the oak
in the hum of the dove

she: I am finished

he: but we
    are just starting

she: are we?

he: first whisper
    of wellness

Athena (Civilizer)

city girl
political woman
wielder of power with the pretty face

incandescent in caves
canyon happy, forest rampant
high on hills

mistress of anger
lightning bolt
from your father's brain

warrior queen
shielding your softness
in breastplate and helmet

an image of battle

that wins the right victories
neither spilling of blood
nor wounding of flesh

your frown
and the trembling of horses
to bring out the best in us

sea god's rival
olive branch plunged into waves

grey-eyed inventor of patterns
weaver of cultures and civil perspectives

bridge between genders

wooing the wily, the restless

travelling light

he: you are magnificent

she: why, because I exercise?

he: because you're fierce

she: like you

he: nothing like me

she: you want a dominatrix

he: no, I want a wisdom figure

she: Liz 1, Golda, Indira, Frau Angela, Hillary

he: I want your force
        not tomboy or sex mate
        sister to me

she: twin to your being

he: what I haven't got

Poseidon (Sea God)

girdle the earth with your ripple of silk
you deep delving power

divide us and bind us

erupting and damaged
our thunder in pieces
a clatter of parts

trample us whole again

new in the salt stream
hoiked high with sea hissings
free as the sails and finned things

alive in the brine
the wings and the smooth gliding eyes

your trident of elements
swaying around us
stately and still

priestly

the waves
in your elegant tresses
bordering lengths of you

strive with Athena for civilization
let olive branch stream with the fishes

in dreams

she: I want to go back to the sea

he: you mean start over

she: start better

he: are you so dissatisfied?

she: the essence eludes us

he: how do you propose...

she: imagine me

he: naked in new ways

she: what are we capable of?

he: my goddess

Leucothia (Sea Mother)

wave-wanderer
garlanding oceans

pusher of tides

sending the breezes
wherever she pleases

plying the waters
with little toy ships
blowing this way and that

spray sparkling fleet ankles
plucking her sailors

from rock-wrecked distress

let us down
          gently

he: on a cruise ship

she: on deck
    my private skiff
    cresting, bucking, cleaving   calmed

    daring the elements

he: yoga classes, casinos and bars

she: days floating the globe's gurgling rim
    we create our ideal
    places

he: yours?

she: when I was young, I skimmed
    the sea in a jumpy little boat

he: and lived to tell the tale

she: loved it, felt every shudder, the air curling
    rocking at night, cradled by sea
    the ping of rope against mast

    singing me to sleep
    ringing me awake

Nephelai (Clouds)

sky walkers
driven by wind

blazing up and blasting

shiver cold spears
run rain to ground

whisper mist

over earth's
    blooming bowl

she: what is it about rain?

he: depressing to some

she: makes me feel clean and new

he: disastrous in parts of the world

she: we've messed with the elements
 upset the balance

he: earth takes its revenge
 turning temperate
 radical

she: will we change?

he: something must

Apollon (Sun Singer)

lyre player in field light
amber-eyed soothsayer

slayer of snakes
swim climb choke
Pytho's harsh land

sacred with sayings

muse maker, chorus leader
comb harmony
through the waves
of your hair

our gaze is one

your rooted sight
soars up through milky flocks
to starry night

time spins under your lash
the chariot fleeing

where wind is up and hissing

notes bloom along your strings
living things accept themselves
seasons chant the scales you sing

threading into each other

she: can you look straight into the sun?

he: only through your eyes

   you look into the sun
   I'll look at you

Pan (Nature)

tune-whistler
season-straddler

nimble forest god
wild speaker

goat-limb, wisp-beard

weave and play
the cave's dark mouth

bubble water through the ground
bounce echoes off sheep backs

spiral eye
ignite the peaks and cast
your beam as far as joy
burning fear

tantalize my dreams

he: panic

she: do you ever?

he: all the time don't we?

she: I'm always anxious

he: at war with ourselves we
frighten everyone

Nymphs (Nature Sprites)

meandering ones
hiding in meadows
leaping with fountains
tripping through streams

trail your veils
of invisible longing
pooling at caverns
covering mountains

reveal yourselves:
dampness on skin
flower from rock

incense cracklers
breathe over us

ash tree dwellers
shower down
your tiny seeds
those drops of blood

our fragile future

live as long as we need
nature

alone and afraid
exhausted and sad

laugh for us, sing for us
how

he: why keep searching?

she: to complete ourselves
    we're not finished

he: how do you know?

she: from those moments that lift me
    every small sharp hint of something
    else

he: voices, a blinding flash?

she: a life at the margins and edges
    inside what's visible
    the silence
    of a single note

Curetes (the Wind Twins)

feather-footed
    whisperers
  a breath
rippling ocean
clearing sky as far as the eye

agile dancers
armed with art
beat the bronze drum
whirl dust into cloud

correct us with fury
when we upset you
agitate depths
root trees in the air
to the hissing of leaves

solace of sailors
push back the storm
that would lay our ship under
a pall of white sea

flute life into being
plants into bloom
distract us with footwork

clash shields over sorrow

out-sing distress

he: so you're a Gemini
you have a history of mischief

she: and benevolence

he: you are named after men

she: beautiful boys, divine young warriors

he: past life?

she: and present

he: how do I know which you is you?

she: you don't
neither do I

he: isn't that confusing?

she: I'm used to it

he: too many choices

she: prevents boredom but

I always want to be
where   and what
I'm not

he: then you're always...

she: restless, yes

he: it will take lifetimes to exhaust the possibilities

she: lifetimes

Horai (the Seasons)

god daughters
cloud gate girls

opening for Olympians
harnessing horses of the sun

replenishing cycles of justice and peace
through conscience, revenge and disaster

sweet-scented, pretty
evergreen census takers

circling the ages

playmates of Persephone
cauterizing flow
in the dead season
firing shut the flesh

dressed only in flowers
dancing life into weathers

that heat it and cool it
melt it and freeze it
burn it and starve it

but always sustain it

she: I wish that justice happened naturally

he: it does...in nature

she: species do attack their own
for survival

he: just like us

she: but we feel relief that we are not the ones
found guilty

he: and call it civilization

she: which is our crime

Artemis (Mother of Transits)

woman of arrows
shooting the moon
changing the light of each night

star-chaser outshining the dark

god's daughter descending

alive at all crossroads
in yellowing noon

awake in shoreline and horizon

mistress of animals
friendly with fawns
horned in the wild

divinity's midwife
engender each day

crouched tight round the palm tree
dazzle soft grass into blossoming women

untangle the young from sweet beds of their birth

amazon of the fields
loosen these ropes and fill up the hollow

pour over seed and multiply me

blaze our best way with the flick
of your time-trailing veil

she: it's exhausting being superwoman

he: so stop

she: what happened to superman?

he: long gone
       faded into twilight

she: the daughter wants a daughter

he: but no mate

she: donor clinic

he: partners primed

she: corn-fed like cattle

he: an old configuration
       still with us

Heracles (Hero)

O masculine man
worker with hands
time toiler, pleasure pusher

tell me my truth

wild beast tamer
children's nurse
self-starter, burly labourer

tasking me to sweat with you
all life's long day

pulling out pain
the branch in your hand
shaking me down
from doubt and dis-ease

shining me round on the ground
pinning me fast

you man-arrow miracle

she: you are heavy

he: Am I hurting you?

she: yes, no

he: I'm sorry
   do you want ...

she: I don't know, just
   be for me

   Nemean Lion, Cretan Bull, Thracian Horse, Arcadian Boar
   the hind of Achaea oh... the stinking stables of Augeas.

he: I will wind you round my waist and wear you well

Persephone (Lost Daughter)

picks a flower in sheer delight
and plunges down

cascaded quickly out of sight
by manic horses eating air
to precious halls and metal light
four months of the year

grieving mother fills the marsh
and waters roots for seasons' harsh
enduring

calling deep below the earth

(with milky breasts and ripened fruit)

by meadow horn

from hiding

her tender sprout
her silky corn
her yellow wheat

she: to hell

he: why are you swearing?

she: because everything good turns bad

he: even, occasionally, conscience

she: will there ever be enough tears
for the mothers of lost children
for the wandering daughters
who barely knew them?

he: bargains can always be made

she: only if you never eat the food of the dead

he: and who can resist that?

Hermes (Communicator)

double deity
snakes entwining the tip
of your sceptre

Hermes here and there

traveller, talker, bargain-maker
selling divine and human
to each other

oracular magician
verbal illusionist

brimmed under sun
winged upon earth
banishing shadow and footprint

phallic athlete, youthful face
adored at pillars and gates

stealing cattle backwards
from under Apollo's nose
stupefying all the eyes of Argus
with your tortoise-shell lyre

trickster, trader
wily with words

persuade us to work and laughter
enrobe our memories with speech

she: you talk too much
      you talk to prove you exist
      you're afraid of silence

he: you write to control

she: that's a lie
      words
          are treacherous

he: so why keep using them?

she: to prove I exist

Dionysus (Creative Chaos)

manic leaper, field-sleeper
earth breaching, face-changing

glitter-barbed moonwalker
break dancer, fire breeder

eater of ecstasy
grape presser
wine maker

bender of genders

masked in the temper of time
buried by secrets
under earth words

stretched upon vines
knotted in sun

     rising
       re-forming

she: he is still with us

he: in our pure adrenalin rush
of war and fun
the same frantic flames

she: savage self-annihilation
performed for those we love

he: keep me
tense between boundary
and breaking

she: divine drunkard
my perfect Attic gentleman

Hephaestus (Divine Worker)

glistening muscle
hammer and anvil
bellows and tongs
hungry flames
drinking light

torso stretched
and shining

twisted wonder
crippled wooer of beauties

flasher, blazer, crafter

fashioning female
bundles of trouble

walking hot coals

heating up mountains
from underground forges
where minerals glow

armouring earth
in flammable sequins

flickering forests
to dazzling extinction

she: could you work in a factory?

he: if I had to

she: all that noise, monotony - deadening!
the fiery forge, that's more like you

he: burning bright

she: my divine worker
drunk on the myth
that pain is purification
or pleasure

sun run with the torch
march it through darkness

feel the flames

he: a lick, a touch
incinerates us

she: trail-blazing glory

Asclepius (Healer)

wed to wellbeing

sprouting green goodness
from malady

a centaur's charge
from spiked forest fringes
whirling torn trees and blunt boulders

but Chiron steps gently
a graceful gait on human toes
draped naked and leaking
warm blood from the kill

Argo sailor

resurrect me in dreams

snaking sacred ways
between us

she: why are we ill?

he: I can't cure you

she: be the doctor
board my feeble craft
blowing into battles with me
watching for wounds

he: beast woman, I'll ride you
drop your warm juices
on my tongue, one
by one, by one

Hygieia (Health)

Green daughter of a doctor
outshone, hiding your light
within garments and hair
adornments of body

Athena's thoughtful favourite

practicing crafts that keep us alive
carefully thriving and flourishing

naked in gymnasia
glistening with athletes
artful figures marking air
muscled boys who stand and fight

sleep by the river on reeds
bathe in winter waters

bearish with pubescent girls
a savagery of innocence
fit and fine to run wild
with men

tame them for marriage

*

he: the body is...

she: a temple...of what, for what?

he: sex, thinking

she: love, imagination

he: and therefore

she: we're back to body

he: the health of...

she: I have no patience with illness

he: you think sickness occurs because somehow it's deserved

she: right

he: so you are responsible for all that happens to you

she: more or less

he: tough being the centre of your world

she: I don't have a choice

he: there's a naturist camp down the road

she: we have our own here
        you flapping around in that kimono like a grand poobah

he: you slipping nude into the pool

she: looking good
        tanned, taut

he: tentative

she: nonchalant

he: cock at half mast

she: asleep in a nest of grey curls
        its own aesthetic

Adonis (Generation)

desired by two

alive in the light
buried by earth-night

fragile flower of broken pots
sprouting on roof-tops
shine and shadow
odourless

little horned burgeoner
bumps on your head
budding seed of both sexes
entangled in hair

jeweled net draping tresses
dark oiled river
all coiled and ready to shoot
for the future

you hunter of happiness
tree springer
                    cheater of death

                withered by goddesses

                    greening the earth

she: it was nice

he: peering down on all the neighbours bickering and barbecuing

she: a son in his sky garden
    almost biblical

he: desert sleep, climbing up at night,
    with bedding after the sun sets

she: vanishing seasons

he: he went blonde, remember?

she: oh yes
    and snapped his hair back in a pony tail
    positively punky

he: your hair always
    thick and crazy
    my Medusa

she: imported from India

he: black gold

she: they are with child

he: fruit of your womb

she: of us

Hippa (Nursemaid of Joy)

pleasure woman
dancing on the mountains
singing in the streets

parading for days
your wine drunk boy
smiling little babe
playing the world
on his flute

boisterous, nocturnal
sacred and sunlit

mirth mother suckle us
save us with ceremonies

bearing your bliss

she: are we expected to be happy all the time?

he: it's not the ultimate value

she: how do we get it into proportion?

he: maybe we think about what 'good' means

she: and how it keeps changing

he: and repeats itself in different forms

she: a kaleidoscope we need to recognize

he: again and again and again

Semele (Dead Mother)

daughter of Cadmus
seeder of cities
men rising from dragon's teeth

deep-bosomed, rope-haired
laid low by lightning

life lady buried
thigh high in divinity

electric in the womb
silvery god bursting out

white hot pain shimmering

rainbows

he: how do you endure childbirth?

she: the oldest and newest female experience

he: pain and joy

she: all mixed up together
agony and ecstasy
fear and excitement
strung out
between life and death

he: you remember

she: every second

Pluton (Lord of the Underworld)

deathless jangler of keys

equal opportunity steward gone underground
sealord and skylord allowing

hide spring in your breathless halls
while the earth sleeps off excess

secret sower of pomegranate seeds
fertilize light

*

he: so, what about death?

she: that's it, the end

he: no afterlife no
    cycles of existence?

she: nature takes care of recycling
    and I'm all for it:
    dust to dust, green grass, fabulous flowers
    the purification of fire

he: but what about soul energy?

she: supply and demand, for example:
    here's Pluton kidnapping Persephone
    amidst stars and leaping deer
    tendrilled plants and soaring birds

    attended by a priapic Hermes
    torso tanned, in sunhat and sandals

he: right, now some vital force had to put all that together

she: it's there:
      she's veiled and demure with perky tits
      he's all damp ebony curls
      positively panting for her

      high stepping horses prance them
      to his golden palace
      where they practice pleasure
      on draped couches
      lobbing red seeds through the air
      cavorting and twittering
      conjuring and sighing
      until the warm weather returns

he: so death is just another way of being

she: if we use our imaginations

he: nobody forced

she: enticed merely
                irresistibly enticed

Charites (the Graces)

deep-bosomed daughters
florid with joy

weaving diaphanous veil
pierced and re-stitched
rent and repaired

sun-rayed and moon-soaked
evergreen glitterers

wedding singers
spinning desire

persuaders of pleasure
radiant rose growers

wafting our love queen
in from the sea

draped over delicate foam
buoyant with Hermes, Poseidon and Eros

dreaming herself alive

she: what is grace?

he: you on the half shell

she: served up and ready to consume
a dash of vinegar, a dab of horseradish
this oyster stings

he: 'hail Venus full of grace'

she: and you

he: carrying all of us

she: oh please

he: oh please do
take us in
make us one
with your...

she: impossible

he: body by Botticelli

Silenus (Wild Man)

hooved and tailed
swift far-seeing

full of father lore
bulbous-bellied with a baby god
bald-headed, vine-wreathed

drunk on drama
donkey wise

ivy-draped grape presser
tufted grinning player
of life over death

with wine, the pipe and the lyre

with lewdness and skill

you marvel of mischief

she: so you're Sag

he: you got it
      your man
      is just a horse's ass

she: beautiful beast, divine animal
       a life force incarnate

he: does that equal human?

she: I envy the instinct of animals

he: we have it

she: dangerous, wouldn't you say?

he: necessary
      creativity lies
      in the balance

she: I'm always falling

he: you're the demon two
      on a tightrope

she: which way will I tip?

he: flip out of the air
      and onto me
      we will ride the flames
      with angel wings

Proteus (Shape Changer)

prophetic old man in the waves

jump-starter
angel-boxer
ghost wrestler

all spume and spray

herding the sea to its pastures
black shiny water dogs
sharp with the bark of their being

storming with form

keeper of time in its moving

creating the ledger of possible things

deciding when
to with-hold, release

deciding what
must go

he: too much choice

she: you'd rather be limited?

he: the responsibility stops me cold

she: it's the agony of the artist
dreadful freedom

and the ecstasy of inhabiting any world
I choose to make

he: take me with you

Melinoe (the Unconscious)

Ripping the womb wide open
mad before she starts
baby princess of the buried self
stuck in winter's lightless world

pale moon waif
terrifying travelers
through the angry night

he: where does evil come from?

she: somebody's child

he: conceived in love

she: programmed by bad seed
      growing along with the good

he: choking it

she: some seed far down, feeding
      on destruction
      alien bud of vengeance
      nourished through seasons
      full of itself, destined to repeat

he: how nourished?

she: if we knew, we'd stop it

he: stop what?

she: the deepest
      darkest parts
      of us

Ares (War)

bloody joy and battle highs
soldier gold
Nike's furious father

ride red
through the planets
trembling like colts
at your flashing

give me war strength
bravery, the sceptre I wield
sharp stick in my hand

glistening killer

wrap your steely limbs
in rosy flesh

and let us love

he: it's no longer possible
to blame men for war

she: it never was
we can start with Helen of Troy
and descend from there
right down to the body parts
of female suicide bombers
bent on heavenly heroics
over male control and serial rape

he: Ares was the father of the Amazons
those cyclopean harpies!
it was a breast not an eye
they traded for arrow accuracy

she: now cancer eats us up

he: cancer is a disease

she: so is war

he: are there no righteous wars?

she: too much is destroyed
we need targeted elimination

he: political assassination
in rare and extreme cases

she: drones kill innocents
while protecting those who kill

and anyway who's to decide?

he: the enlightened ones

she: who know...?

he: who knows...

she: what makes us
human?

127

Ino (Reversal)

deep-bosomed goddess
of delicate ankle

daughter of Cadmus

speeding stern winds
stirring up tides

suckling the wild god

madly tormenting your own son
you leap off high rocks
with him dead, then alive
on sleek speeding dolphins
and popular worship

you jealously torture new seeds
into famine and flee undersea

where you swim to Odysseus, wave-wending
wrecked in his ship on the coast
of your rescue

mother of fortune
and fate

she: motherhood is not peaceful

he: like the lake

she: baby girl strung tight
curled small on the floor
in tantrums
flung into far corners

he: see the smelt fishers
and their wide white nets

she: hear them
rattling light in the night

he: little boy
whining his pain
so much it just hurts

she: and you
addicted to everything bad, daily
giving and spending yourself

coming up empty
under startled trees

Diké (Justice)

god's policewoman
shining watcher of the tribes

sailing the mind that stops
at no shore
symmetry leaping
down on injustice
hammer in hand
to pound out the ugly

filling the cave with new stirrings
rumours and sightings
no priest could imagine

nor despot prevent

he: eventually she fled to heaven
      and became the constellation, Virgo

she: became my first husband

he: what!

she: he was a Virgo, virginal
       untouched and too good for me

he: and when you made love?

she: love purified the act

he: and when you gave yourself to me?

she: spiritual transgression
       the ultimate evil

he: what was his sin, then?

she: not sailing seas with me

Nomus (Natural Law)

invisible acrobat
of the
visible world

settling stars
smoothing seas

a flash between
there and here

blazing trail
from remote cosmic storms

to a spider's fine stitch
the bee in a flower
moon howl of a wolf
and twitching unease

help us survive all disaster

the flood of foundations
that drowned mountaintops
through air turning water
and lifeboats like leaves

let us dry dock at last
on green peaks
of your knowing

he: do you understand
how things work?

she: some things

he: electricity for instance?

she: protons and electrons
but it's not my field

he: is it all explained?

she: there's just too much
so intricate, complex, delicate, inter-connected

he: how does it all keep going?

she: we are complicit

he: yes

she: we have some sacred duty
to pay attention

as it lives and breathes
rests and heaves
carrying us through

sloughing us off
if for a moment
we look away

Nomus (Universal Law)

setting stars in order

woven into the world
but not of it

marching the animals two by two
on long cosmic leashes

hauling up the waters
seeping through foundations

high-climbing floods
bringing far flung mountains
close as mosaics
curling on sea floors

snow cools the eddies
that spin a hollow ark
in air, whirling water

soft thud   down
on a single ancient peak

drying under sun

beginning again

she: what if there is another force
some manic conductor experimenting
with every variety of cataclysm
in the service of a perfect hidden pattern
what if...

he: nonsense

she: what if
neither science nor environmental abuse can explain it away?

he: you're saying
this same fanatical order
that studs the night sky
shoves tides around their salty beds
shrinks and balloons the moon

this insatiability

when certainty gets boring
simply stirs things up

because it can?

she: and maybe because

we're supposed to learn something

The Muses (Inspiration)

enchant the beast and charm the rock
delight the trees

oh Epic, Historic, Lyric and Choral
Tragical, Comical, Hymnic and Mimicking
Astronomical, always

make music the law

record and remember
flood, ice, volcano
all the weathers
of our worlds

nursed in your hospital

green park of artists
writing on air
archiving the stories
in quick-frozen dance

divinely contemptuous

know how we need you
magpies deplumed
blundering, blind

give us the lyre
to hear every harmony

quiver the strings
tremble the fabric
draping the form

tilt-tap the toes

your sparkling crescendos
will ribbon our night

she: what good is art?
　　　wouldn't it be more useful
　　　to make babies, prepare food?

he: some are born to nurture images
　　　see our world differently

she: really?

he: it's a creative act, new every time

she: I'm afraid of getting stuck
　　　　on repeat

he: you won't
　　　as long as I
　　　keep you
　　　a-mused

Moirai (the Fates)

night's love goddesses
Zeus spume flying clear
over water, dropped hot
into the sculpted stone
we call life

destiny riders in lilac dresses
spun round the sun track
of world weathers
flaring, equally foul
and fair

circling fatal plains
in god's global eye

sure as the swing of time

                  measured

                          cut

she: we don't know our destiny

he: so why believe in it?

she: each life is different
  follows its own pattern

he: pre-determined?

she: somehow, yes
  and death comes for all of us

he: we can change our destiny

she: can we?
  can we do more than
  follow free will?

he: what keeps us going?

she: not knowing

About the Author

Patricia Keeney is an award-winning poet, novelist, theatre and literary critic. Born in the UK to a Canadian father and a British mother, she moved to Canada with her parents at the age of three and grew up in Ottawa and Montreal. A graduate of McGill University, she later did doctoral studies in the UK subsequently returning to Canada where she began teaching Creative Writing and English at Toronto's York University.

A well-known critic for many years for CBC Radio, *Canadian Forum*, *Scene Changes*, *Canadian Theatre Review* and *Canadian Literature*, she continues her critical work both nationally and internationally in journals such as *Arc* and online, *Critical Stages* and *Critically Speaking*.

Keeney began publishing her own poetry in Canadian journals and magazines in the late 1980s. In 1988, her first collection of poetry, *Swimming Alone* attracted serious critical attention prompting the British poet Ted Hughes to praise her "very natural voice" and "the real life burning away in these poems." Now the author of ten books of poetry and two novels, her poetry has been translated and published in French (winning the Prix Jean Paris in 2003), Spanish, Bulgarian, Chinese and Hindi while her *Selected Poems* carries an introduction by the distinguished Russian poet Yevgeny Yevtushenko.

She describes her latest volume, *Orpheus in Our World* as an exercise in poetic archeology connecting the earliest and rarely translated Greek hymns with a post-modern theatrical dialogue. "Yes," she says, "these pieces can be read aloud like the ancient Greek hymns and played theatrically like ancient Greek drama." Coming into print at almost the same time as this volume is Keeney's latest novel, *One Man Dancing* (Inanna) – a very personal human and political adventure based on the true story of a Ugandan actor who became a political refugee in Canada after almost being assassinated by Idi Amin while working for Africa's most experimental theatre company, Abafumi. An avid traveller, Keeney has taught and lectured in Europe, Africa and Asia. *See Patricia Keeney's website: Wapitiwords. ca.*

NeoPoiesis: *a new way of making*

1) in ancient Greece, poiesis referred to the process of making: creation - production - organization - formation - causation

2) a process that can be physical and spiritual, biological and intellectual, artistic and technological, material and teleological, efficient and formal

3) a means of modifying the environment and a method of organizing the self, the making of art and music and poetry, the fashioning of memory and history and philosophy, the construction of perception and expression and reality

4) an independent publisher with a steadfast goal to print and promote outstanding poets, writers and artists that reflect the creative drive and spirit of the new electronic landscape

NeoPoiesisPress.com